Kiki Dee is Gluten-Free

Written by Jennifer Ostmann | Illustrated by Jasmine Bailey
©2020 Lemon Lady Press LLC

Copyright © 2020 by Jennifer Ostmann

All rights reserved. This book or any portion thereof may not be reproduced or used in any manner whatsoever without the express written permission of the publisher except for the use of brief quotations in a book review.

Printed in the United States of America
First Printing, 2020

ISBN 978-0-578-70752-5

Lemon Lady Press
Milwaukee, WI 53217
www.lemonladypress.com

*To Kathryn Grace, you are one tough cookie
(gluten-free, of course) and an inspiration to me.
I love you, Kiki Pie!*

Whipped cream clouds dance across the sky.
Kiki plays soccer with Pumpkin nearby.

Cookies, waffles, and strawberry pies
Are all that can be seen in this little girl's eyes.

Donuts with icing and sprinkles are oh, so pretty.
But they are not kind to Kiki like a sweet, gentle kitty.

These treats contain ingredients like gluten and wheat.
Kiki cannot bear them, not even one treat.

They make her feel icky, rotten to the core;
However, celery and all things green are such a bore!

"How can this be?" Kiki sobs and cries.
"How can these desserts be such a lie?"

Meanwhile, peanut butter, fluff, and fondue are happy they are in the clear.
These yummy spreads take to the sidelines to smile and cheer.

Forks march in anticipating delight,
But the sugary bunch is ready to fight.

"We're tasty, pleasing, fruity, and sweet,"
Miss Macaroon hollers on repeat.

Shortbread cookies start to crumble while sauce finds the noodles. Salty are the pretzels, and tart is the lemon strudel.

Distant is the time of cookies n' cream.
Cheesy fish crackers are yesterday's dream.

"I'm hungry," Kiki bellows. "I just want a snack.
My tummy is rumbling; can't we go back?
Remember, how things were before my condition?
You all played a special part in this marvelous kitchen."

"My sandwiches have been smothered with jam,
And gluten-free crackers can be topped with ham.

I use to eat cones, but sundaes will do.
Maybe this is something I had to go through!"

"You can stay if you want or leave if you choose,
But nobody here will win or lose."

Teams begin to organize; it is wheat vs. the rest.
The food mashes and strains to see which ones are best.

Wow! What a messy surprise!
They can't believe their eyes.
In the end, it is a draw; no snack wins the game.
Kiki sighs, "If only you were more of the same."

"What an idea!" Cheese says. "We can find a new fit!"
The foods mix to create grain-free snacks that are a hit.

"Rice Pasta, step up" says Cheese to the Mac.
"Popcorn, move to the front, and Grahams to the back!"

"I can make pizza," says Mr. Cauliflower to Cheese.
Miss Pineapple calls, "Let's remain in sight," to Sugar Snap Peas.

Kiki smiles and thinks of Granny, who drinks almond milk instead of dairy.
Miss Winny, her teacher, is allergic to cherries.

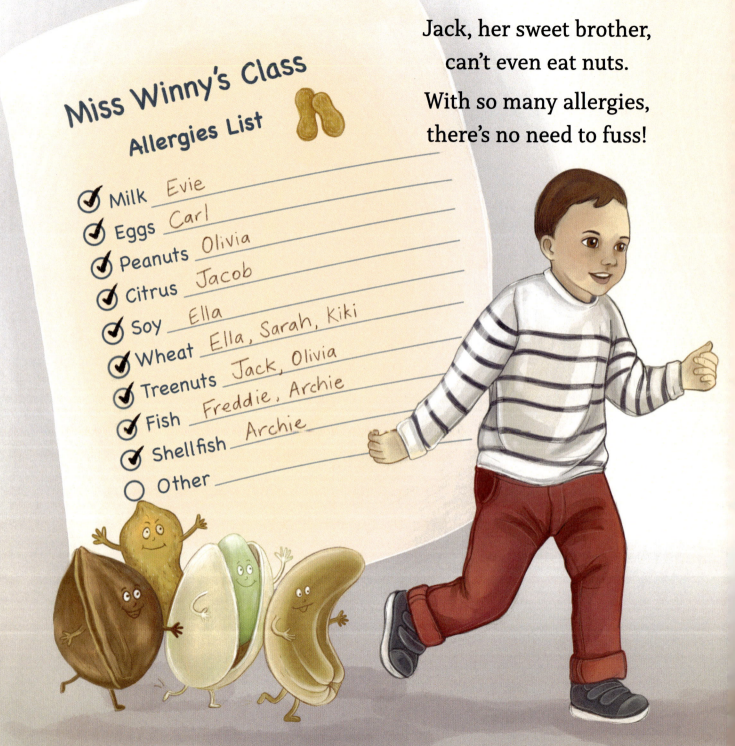

While at school, Kiki Dee smiles at her colorful plate.
She can't have gluten, and that is not a bad fate.

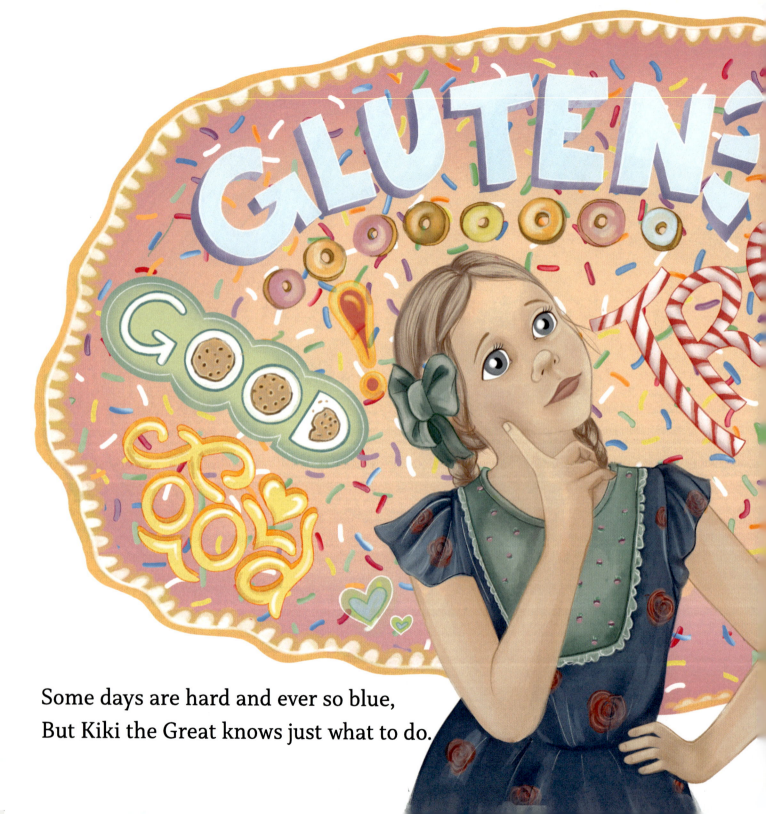

Some days are hard and ever so blue,
But Kiki the Great knows just what to do.

Kiki knows she isn't alone in the battle with food.
She keeps her chin up and brightens her mood.

"No more days sick in bed!" she shouts with glee.

Even birthday parties can be gluten-free!

About the Author:

Jennifer Ostmann has more than ten years' experience in elementary education with a master's degree in reading specialties and learning disabilities. Her highest honors include being a mama to two active kiddos and wife to the best human she knows. When her five-year-old daughter began to struggle with her gluten-free diet, Jennifer decided to write a book to help Kate become her own self advocate. Unfortunately, there have never been any known food fights in Jennifer's cozy Whitefish Bay, Wisconsin kitchen; however, she claims (after many mishaps) to now make the best gluten-free brownies in town. You can visit Jennifer online at www.lemonladypress.com.

Made in the USA
Coppell, TX
21 November 2020